I0814272

Unicorns

by Grace Hansen

Abdo Kids Jumbo is an Imprint of Abdo Kids
abdobooks.com

abdobooks.com

Published by Abdo Kids, a division of ABDO, P.O. Box 398166, Minneapolis, Minnesota 55439.

Printed in the United States of America, North Mankato, Minnesota.

052022

092022

Photo Credits: Alamy, Getty Images, Granger Collection, Shutterstock, ©Wellcome Images p.13/CC BY 4.0

Production Contributors: Teddy Borth, Jennie Forsberg, Grace Hansen
Design Contributors: Candice Keimig, Pakou Moua

Library of Congress Control Number: 2021950547

Publisher's Cataloging-in-Publication Data

Names: Hansen, Grace, author.

Title: Unicorns / by Grace Hansen.

Description: Minneapolis, Minnesota : Abdo Kids, 2023 | Series: World of mythical beings | Includes online resources and index.

Identifiers: ISBN 9781098261917 (lib. bdg.) | ISBN 9781098262754 (ebook) | ISBN 9781098263171 (Read-to-Me ebook)

Subjects: LCSH: Unicorns--Juvenile literature. | Mythical animals--Juvenile literature. | Folklore--Juvenile literature. | Legends--Juvenile literature.

Classification: DDC 398.24--dc23

Table of Contents

Myth of the Unicorn

Unicorns are wondrous mythical beings. Unicorn legends from certain times and places describe different creatures. But in most stories, all unicorns have a magical horn.

Eastern Unicorns

Unicorns have appeared in many cultures. In Chinese mythology, the unicorn is known as the *qilin*. It can look like a **calf** with scales and a horn. In other myths, it has antlers and a dragon's head.

Myths about the *qilin* say that it can bring people to and from heaven. Today, the *qilin* is mainly a symbol of good luck and protection.

In Japan, the unicorn is known as the *kirin.* It has a deer's body and a dragon's head. The *kirin* can be shown with antlers or a horn. It is kind and shy, and a symbol of **purity**.

Western Unicorns

Ctesias was a Greek historian and physician. He wrote a book in 430 BCE about India and the things that live there. One was a creature that looked like a colorful donkey with a horn.

By the Middle Ages, new unicorn legends appeared. In **medieval** myths, the creatures look more like horses. They are beautiful, strong, and glow in the moonlight.

Unicorns are shy and gentle. But they fight bravely when they have to. They also protect other creatures and humans.

A unicorn's horn is called an alicorn. It is magical and can **pierce** any material. Up until the 18th century, people believed the horn of a unicorn could heal the sick.

Like in Asian cultures, English kings and queens used the unicorn as a symbol of goodness. The unicorn is still shown this way in stories today.

Royal coat of arms of the United Kingdom

Other Mythical Creatures

Centaur

- From Greek mythology
- The lower body of a horse with the upper body of a human
- Wild but can also possess great **wisdom**

Griffin

- A powerful and majestic creature that appears in many mythologies including Greek, Roman, and Egyptian
- **Hybrid** of a lion and an eagle
- Guards treasures

Faun

- From Greek and Roman mythology
- Legs and tail of a goat and the upper body of a man
- Often shown with horns and pointed ears
- A symbol of peace

Phoenix

- A legendary bird in many mythologies, including Egyptian and Greek
- Known for bursting into flame at the end of its life only to rise from its ashes
- A symbol of **immortality** and rebirth

Glossary

calf - a young cow or bull.

hybrid - a mixture of two or more things to make one new thing.

immortality - the state or condition of living forever.

medieval - of or having to do with the Middle Ages.

pierce - to go through; to make a hole in.

purity - the state or quality of being without sin or guilt.

wisdom - good judgment and an understanding of that which is true or good.

Index

Visit **abdokids.com** to access crafts, games, videos, and more!

Use Abdo Kids code

WUK1917

or scan this QR code!